This book belongs to:

____

Made in the USA
Coppell, TX
16 September 2022

83252734R00066